Still Me

Finding Yourself Again in the Caregiver's Journey

BY SHELLIE STARK

Dedication

To every caregiver who has forgotten themselves in the process of showing up for someone else. May you be reminded: You are still here. And you are still you.

To my mommy Diana, thank you for giving me the most fulfilling opportunity I will receive in this lifetime. The gift to serve and to honor the woman who cultivated the light, resilence and pure heart within me.

Caring for you revealed my purpose:

To stand in the gap without allowing myself to disappear, to witness love in its truest form, to hold space where strength and surrender meet, and to remind others that devotion does not require self-erasure.

This journey shaped my voice, anchored my faith, and clarified my assignment—to speak for those who are tired, unseen, and quietly enduring; to illuminate the sacred work of caregiving; and to affirm that even in sacrifice, identity remains.

This book is my obedience. My testimony. My return.

And for every soul learning how to serve with love while staying whole.

Table of Contents

MOMENT 01
　A Love That Heals and Hurts 11

MOMENT 02
　The Silent Spiral—When Caregiving Takes Over 23

MOMENT 03
　The Turning Point: Realizing You Are Still Here 29

MOMENT 04
　Redefining Strength: The Power of Saying
　"I Need Help" 35

MOMENT 05
　Building Your Support Circle Without Asking 41

MOMENT 06
　Creating Boundaries in the Midst of Care 47

MOMENT 07
　Building a Respite Routine 53

MOMENT 08
　Self-Care Isn't Selfish: It's Survival 59

MOMENT 09
    Letting Go of Guilt: You Deserve Rest 65

MOMENT 10
    Finding Your Joy Again 71

MOMENT 11
    Building a Sustainable Life Beyond the Crisis 77

MOMENT 12
    When You're Ready to Let Go 83

MOMENT 13
    Grief, Growth, and Grace 89

MOMENT 14
    Reflections from Other Caregivers 95

MOMENT 15
    Journal Section: Your Space to Be Seen 101

    Resource Toolkit 125

How to Use This Journal: A Note Before You Begin

Dear Caregiver,

Before we begin, I want you to know—this isn't just a book. It's a companion.

Each moment holds part of my story, but just as importantly, it's designed to hold space for yours. At the end of every moment, you'll find daily affirmations, journal prompts, and practical tools. These aren't just extras—they're the reason I can even share this story with you today.

The affirmations helped me breathe on days I forgot how.

The prompts gave my pain somewhere safe to land.

The tools? They brought me back to myself—one small action at a time.

I included these for you so that this book doesn't just speak to you—it speaks with you. This is a living, breathing space of healing. A soft nudge back to the person you may have set aside while showing up for someone else.

You'll see lines where you can write directly in the book—but I encourage you to also keep a personal journal nearby. Some reflections deserve room to stretch. Some truths need privacy before they're ready to be spoken aloud. Your journal is your sacred space—use it freely, honestly, and without judgment.

This journey we're on together isn't about doing it "right." It's about remembering yourself through each page. One breath, one question, one small act of care at a time.

Pause when you need. Revisit when you must. And most of all—honor your truth as it rises.

With love,

Shellie

Introduction:

If you really want to know the heart of this book, you must know the heart of me—and the woman who gave me mine.

I am the only child of a woman who loved me with everything she had, even when she didn't have much in the physical sense to give. A woman who stayed when her own mother didn't. A woman who was told she would never conceive and prayed for a child of her own. She carried the weight of her siblings and community while still finding a way to laugh with me, cry with me, and teach me how to be tender and strong at the same time. We are more than mother and daughter—we are soul sisters, a reflection of each other, side by side.

Growing up, we were often in a state of survival mode. Homeless at one point. Bounced between homes. And still, my mother never let go of my hand. I have her heart, and she has mine. I watched her sacrifice silently, often putting others before herself, and unknowingly, she taught me to do the same. She was 26 when she gave birth to me. I was 26 when I brought her into the life I built after a decade of healing and growing on my own. I wanted to give her a new world—a world where we could finally thrive, not just survive.

But I didn't expect that our joined worlds would become a new moment of caregiving. I didn't expect the hospital stays, the medications, the endless battles with a system that too often failed us. I didn't expect the fear. Or the sacredness. Or the strength, I didn't know I had.

What began as a gift to her—to show her the life I had built—became a journey that tested every part of me. There have been days I've felt buried in responsibilities. Alone in a room full of people. Forgotten in my own life. But through it all, the one thing I've never lost is love. The kind that shows up even when no one else does. Disciplined, effortless, and a shield of protection. The kind she gave me, and I now give back to her, day after day.

This journal was born from that journey. It's not just a collection of thoughts. It's a mirror. A soft place to land. A reminder that even when you feel like you're disappearing, you are still here. You are still you.

Inside these pages, you'll find pieces of my story—but more importantly, you'll find space for your own. Because caregiving is sacred. It's exhausting. It's beautiful and brutal all at once. And you deserve somewhere to unpack it all.

You'll walk with me through moments of awakening, grief, joy, resentment, restoration, and release. And I'll offer you tools, reflections, affirmations, and the kind of questions that help you find yourself again.

Because if I've learned anything, it's this: roles may shift, but who we are is still sacred. I may now be the protector, and she the one who leans on me—but in many ways, she's still my safe space. And this book? It's my offering to others walking the same invisible path.

If you are tired, this is for you.

If you are grieving, this is for you.

If you are holding it all together for everyone else, this is especially for you. Come with me. Let's walk this journey together. Let's remember who we are. Let's find our way back home to ourselves.

Because you are not alone.

And you are still here.

MOMENT 1

A Love That Heals and Hurts

Sitting at the foot of a hospital bed alone, being told you might have to prepare a funeral. Immediately, the fight of advocating began in the midst of uncertainty, and my inner child desperately needed a hug. As an only child, this was always one of my greatest concerns. I remember saying, "I am not ready to lose my mother". In that moment, I pleaded in tears with Yah to allow me to endure because it is better than having to endure the loss.

Now, I ask, is one ever ready to be of service or a caregiver? What did "endure" really mean compared to responsibilities? How does someone even decide or become chosen for such a highly regarded and undervalued role? While there are many types of caregivers in our society, I believe it ultimately comes down to having the heart to be of service to something or someone outside of oneself.

I never knew my journey would evolve into a full-time career in caregiving, and it has completely changed my life.

Having the weight of what feels like a war zone, fighting healthcare professionals to achieve results to gain answers. Some would call it advocating, but when you are already emotionally depleted and capacity levels are low, it appears as a fight.

When my mom had her stroke, I pushed for them to give her an MRI. It wasn't until I spoke with the third doctor who agreed to run the test. I said to her, "If this were your mother, wouldn't you want to turn over every rock"? Her response, "That's fair." Wow, "that's fair" could seem so meaningless to most, but in that moment, it was as if I won a gold medal at the Olympics. Rather, this is a life we are speaking of here, and whether someone lives or dies. It came down to a short phrase, "that's fair." After getting back the results, we had an answer of stroke and heart attack. Then the real journey began.

I knew if I was carrying this weight in silence, there were many others doing the same thing. But nobody is talking about it, they just do it. Regardless of whether they have the full capacity or not. If I can help one person understand themselves as a healer and learn how to heal themselves through the journey, then I am forever grateful for the purpose that has been gifted to me in sharing my own story. Leaning in and learning how to be of service to myself has always been my responsibility.

This is the reason I am coming from behind the veil, out of the silent shadows, to share my personal story in hopes that it inspires and empowers others to unmask, look in the mirror, and do the same.

When the time comes, there was no hesitation—only actionable love, and the quiet knowing that this was mine to carry. What I didn't anticipate was the cost. Not just financially, but emotionally, spiritually, and physically.

This guided book is for every caregiver who feels lost in the spiral, who has forgotten their own name in service to someone they love or has been called to serve. You are not alone.

We begin by acknowledging the power; beauty of the caregiver's heart—and the toll it can take over time. Understanding this duality is essential to healing.

There's a unique intimacy in caring for someone who depends on you. It's a bond forged in necessity and love. You witness their vulnerability. You become their voice, their advocate, their memory, their hands. That love is real, but so is the exhaustion. There will be times when you may clash with the person you are caring for because they rebel against the grain. The thought of losing control is difficult for them. They don't realize that what you are doing is ultimately to help them, but it appears to them as if they no longer have control over their decisions, choices, or way of life. So, the exhaustion can feel like you are fighting on all sides, medically and emotionally, with your loved one.

Remember your why; this will allow you to continue forging ahead by showing up every day and not quitting. There were times during the hospitalization when she did not eat. They wanted to give her a feeding tube, and I knew my mom's wishes. I had faith she would get the nutrients that she needed. From the time we woke up, I would feed her meal supplements in a 3-oz cup from sunrise to 9 pm or 10 pm at night. While the journey was fueled by love, it also complicated it. There were decisions I made, such as not choosing to put her on a feeding, out of an emotional response to honoring her wish.

In this moment, we'll walk together through the heart of what caregiving looks like—beyond the medical charts and to-do lists. We'll talk about what no one prepares you for: the moment you realize your life has quietly shifted beneath your feet, and you're not sure how to step forward. I will share my lived experiences, lessons learned, and conquering healing tips.

Caregiving didn't knock on my door with a warning. It showed up quietly. First, as emotional support, then transitioned suddenly due to a diagnosis. That turned into errands, then check-ins,

and soon it swallowed my schedule, dictating every decision—beginning as a young person in life.

I remember working a corporate job in my early twenties with a desire to climb the corporate ladder and receiving passive aggressive reprisal because I would have to take off to either care for or take my parent to doctors' appointments. I vividly remember two occasions that would change my perspective on working for others. A colleague from the office said, "Are you really taking care of your mother?" as if I was lying about my responsibilities.

I knew that I was in a toxic work environment when my mother went into the hospital and had surgery. She ended up having an obstruction, and I needed to be her advocate, so I wanted to be by her side. I requested to work from the hospital and was told, verbatim, by HR, "She's in the hospital, isn't that the best place for her to get care, why do you need to be there?" I was appalled and taken aback, and in that moment, I realized I was sacrificing precious time I may never get back for a dollar. It was in that moment that I decided I would not trade making money for memorable moments.

I later tranistioned into tv and film which allow me the flexibility to adjust my schedule. Although, it was also demanding due to travel requirements. During the pandemic I became a guided meditation instructor then later working remote and recently experienced an employer who was compassionate and understanding. Offering caregiving assistance within the benefits. A complete stark difference from what I had edured at a young age caregiver. I am truly grateful I was able to experience a company who shows they care by their actions. Perhaps you have had a similar experience as well. Or maybe it was hidden in obligations, such as having a child, deciding to work in the healthcare industry, or caring for a loved one because of the relationship, not realizing the call you are answering is to be a healer. qWhatever your story, your path to caregiving may have started out of love—but it also brought weight. And that weight, if not named, begins to shape your sense of identity. You become "the strong one," "the dependable one," "the one who knows what meds are due."

But who sees you?

What No One Talks About

No one talks about the loneliness. The resentment you feel for missing out on normal things—coffee dates, vacations, even a full night's sleep. The grief of watching someone you love slip away. Learning the lesson that you do not have control over it. The guilt of wanting a break. I became a planner because I wanted to travel the world, but also to ensure that things were taken care of while I was away. Every decision I make, and continue to make, is with caregiving in mind.

And then there's the silence. The world doesn't see the labor behind caregiving. There are no medals, no ceremonies. Just another day of showing up while your soul whispers, "Don't forget me."

Spiritual Anchoring in the Storm

Caregiving will crack you open—emotionally, mentally, and spiritually. And yet, in the cracks, light can enter. This moment invites you to reflect on what grounds you. Is it faith? Prayer? Breathwork? Meditation?

For me, there were moments I could only whisper a prayer or say nothing at all while standing in the bathroom, hiding tears.

There were mornings I held onto scriptures or affirmations just to get through breakfast.

Caregiving invites us deeper—not because we want it, but because we need it. It strips away distractions. It calls for surrender. I truly believe that when we are called to an assignment in life, it is by design. Too much is given, much will be required. Luke 12:48

Now, there is a second part to that, and it is "and to whom men have committed much, of him they will ask the more. My interpretation is, you have been chosen and entrusted to hold such responsibility to a higher standard and will be rewarded for using the gift that was placed inside of you.

The Caregiver's Body: Carrying the Weight

Let's be honest: it's not just your heart that hurts. Your body carries the fatigue. Tension in your shoulders, sleepless nights, skipped meals, or even overeating. The aches that show up as your body's quiet protest.

If your body could speak, what would it say?

This section offers a simple self-check:

- Have I eaten a full meal today?
- Have I stretched or breathed deeply?
- Have I had water?

Sometimes, survival means going back to the basics.

Love as Both Balm and Burden

Yes, love fuels this journey—but it can also complicate it. You love the person you're caring for, but that doesn't mean every moment feels loving. You may feel frustrated, angry, and bitter. That doesn't make you a bad caregiver. It makes you human.

We need to normalize those feelings. We'll explore tools to process complex emotions without shame.

Your Worth Outside the Role

You are more than what you do for others. You have dreams, desires, and needs that are valid even when someone else's needs seem more urgent. Your worth is not measured by how much you give away.

In this section, we'll reflect on the following:

- Who were you before caregiving?
- What did you love?
- What dreams have been paused, not erased?

We will practice reclaiming those truths.

A Gentle Invitation

Let this moment be your pause. Let it be your reminder. You are seen, and you are sacred. This work you do—this sacred, invisible labor—it matters. But so do you.

And you are still here.

Let's breathe. Let's remember. Let's begin.

You might even start resenting the very person you love. And then the shame sets in. "What kind of person feels this way?" Especially when they are being difficult and resistant to healing, and not doing the things that help them heal. It makes it harder because you may feel like you want them to live more than they are willing to put in the work to do so. Let me tell you: a human one.

Daily Affirmations

- I am still here, even in the midst of change.

- I honor the love that drives me and strength it takes to continue.

- I release fear and make room for compassion—toward myself.

- I am more than what I carry.

- I can tell my story, and I am allowed to be seen.

Journal Prompts

1. What was the moment I realized I had become a caregiver?

----

2. What have I not allowed myself to grieve?

----

3. How has caregiving shaped how I see myself?

----

4. What does love look like for me when I turn it inward?

This moment is just the beginning. Let's keep going—together.

MOMENT 2

The Silent Spiral—When Caregiving Takes Over

No one tells you how fast it can happen. One day you're juggling work, life, maybe a social calendar—and the next, you're knee- deep in appointments, paperwork, sleepless nights, and emotions you can't quite name.

It starts slowly—this spiral. You don't even notice it at first. You're just helping. A doctor's visit here. A late-night phone call there. A quick favor, a ride to an appointment, picking up a prescription. Then suddenly, you look up, and your entire life has shifted.

You've stopped answering texts. You cancel plans more than you keep them. You show up late to gatherings, acting as though you hadn't just cried before arriving. The hobbies you loved are distant memories. You don't remember the last time you had a

real night's sleep. You are exhausted, but you keep going because that's what you do. That's what I did.

I didn't know I was losing myself. I thought I was just being responsible. I thought I was doing the right thing. And I was—but at the cost of forgetting me.

I began saying "yes" to everything—out of guilt, out of fear, out of love. I filled every gap, covered every detail, and made every call. The spiral doesn't look like chaos to anyone else. To the outside world, it may seem like you have it all together.

Inside, you're unraveling.

The silent spiral is dangerous not because it's loud, but because it's quiet. Because it convinces you that this is just the way it is now. That you're selfish if you want a break. That everyone else's needs come first. That this is what good daughters, sons, spouses, and siblings do.

It's not just the tasks. It's the constant anticipation. The mental checklist that never turns off. The waiting for the next symptom, phone call, or emergency. It's living in a heightened state of alert so long that you forget what it's like to breathe fully.

Sometimes I'd cry in the car after errands. Sometimes I'd find myself staring at the wall while reheating dinner praying my loved one would eat this time. My body was present, but my spirit was somewhere curled up, tired and unheard.

And yet, the world applauds your dedication. They call you strong. They don't see the breaking.

What I needed was someone to ask me how I was—really. What I needed was for someone to see me beneath the cape and intentional show to give me a hug.

So I began asking myself that question.

And in that honest space, I started writing again. Not for anyone else. Just for me. Just to get the noise out of my head. I began walking in silence, without music or podcasts, just listening to the sound of my feet on the pavement.

These became the breadcrumbs back to myself.

This moment is about awakening. About seeing the spiral. Naming it. Gently, without judgment.

It's about realizing that just because caregiving is hard doesn't mean you have to lose yourself to it.

Daily Affirmations to Break the Spiral

- I am allowed to be more than what I do for others.

- My exhaustion is not a weakness. It is a signal.

- I deserve care, too.

- Saying "no" can be sacred.

- My needs matter, even if they feel invisible.

Journal Prompts

1. When was the last time I felt like myself?

---

2. What have I stopped doing that once brought me joy?

---

3. Where in my day can I pause for five minutes?

---

4. Who could I reach out to—even just to say "I'm not okay"?

Tools That Helped Me Step Out of the Spiral

- Setting a timer to remind myself to eat or stretch
- Leaving one chore undone on purpose to rest instead
- Creating a small corner of my home just for peace
- Letting people in—mess and all

You are not failing by feeling overwhelmed. You are not weak for needing space. You are not selfish for wanting to feel like yourself again.

The spiral can be interrupted. The silence can be broken. And your identity can be remembered. You are still here. You are still worthy. And it's not too late to come back to yourself.

MOMENT 3

The Turning Point: Realizing You Are Still Here

This moment marked the moment when everything changed for me. It was the day I realized I didn't have to live in constant fear or obligation. I had the power to redefine what strength meant. This moment delves into how I transitioned from feeling overwhelmed and afraid to recognizing that I was still present and worthy of care.

The transition didn't come all at once. It began with noticing the exhaustion, resentment, and numbness. It started with tiny acts of self-compassion—letting myself sleep in an extra hour, not answering every phone call, and speaking gently to myself. Putting my phone on Do Not Disturb.

Imagine waking up and being unable to feel one side of your body. Well, that was what happened to me. I woke up and my entire left side was numb. I had tingling in my feet, and my lower back was extremely sore. My body was ultimately screaming for help. I had no choice but to respond. I was driving, and the pain became unbearable.

This was a result of lifting my mom multiple times a day. I am strong, standing at a whopping 4'10" in height and weighing a solid 140 pounds. My mom, on the other hand, standing 5'6 in height and now a solid 178lbs. While I am grateful, she has gained weight since it was a journey to get her to eat. I am now lifting more weight on my frame. I immediately knew something needed to shift. My body needed some love before it tapped out. I made an appointment with one of my bestfriends, a chiropractor, which marked the start of my transition back.

It wasn't easy. There were and have been days I reverted into old patterns, thinking I had to earn rest or prove my love through exhaustion. But over time, I began to trust that I was not abandoning my loved one by caring for myself—I was becoming a better, more present version of myself.

This was my turning point: when I chose to be still and ask myself hard questions.

- Who am I without this title?
- What do I miss about myself?
- What small thing could I reclaim today?

I started slowly, lighting a candle in the mornings, listening to music I loved, and walking barefoot in the grass to remind myself that I was human, not just a function.

I had to forgive myself for being tired. For being angry. For wanting a break.

And I had to learn that even in the midst of care-taking, I could still find pockets of joy. That even if I couldn't leave the house, I could leave the heaviness. Even for a moment.

Practical Tools
That Helped Me Reconnect with Myself:

- Scheduled "sacred 15" minutes daily with no expectations.
- Replaced one "I have to" thought with "I get to choose".
- Wrote myself permission slips: "You are allowed to rest".
- Created a grounding practice using breath and touch (placing a hand over my heart).

Daily Affirmations

- I am more than what I do.
- I am still worthy, even when I am tired.
- I honor both my love and my limits.
- My identity is sacred.

Journal Prompts

1. What did I used to love before caregiving?

------

2. What part of myself am I ready to welcome back?

------

3. What's one thing I can do for me this week?

You are not only a caregiver. You are still a dreamer, a thinker, a creative, a soul. The turning point isn't about quitting—it's about remembering.

You are still here. You are still you.

MOMENT 4

Redefining Strength: The Power of Saying "I Need Help"

I used to believe strength meant handling everything on my own. I was the one who showed up for everyone else, who figured things out, who never cracked even when the weight became unbearable. The idea of asking for help felt like failure—like weakness.

But caregiving will teach you things about yourself that nothing else will. It will peel back the layers of pride and reveal where you're bleeding, where you're breaking, and where you desperately need to be held.

For the longest time, I waited for someone to notice I needed help. I thought if they really cared, they'd just offer. The truth is, most people are so wrapped in their own lives they don't see the unraveling unless we name it. And naming it? That's not a weakness. That's courage.

It took me years to whisper the words, "I need help." But the moment I did, something shifted. I wasn't alone anymore. And that changed everything.

This moment is about redefining what strength looks like. It's about understanding that vulnerability isn't the opposite of strength—it is the gateway to it. Text message from me, "Hey y'all, I hope your day is amazing. Things have been really hard taking care of mom by myself. I know everyone has a life, but if you have a moment, could you stop by to sit with her? That would be wonderful. I know she would enjoy seeing you, and it would also give me time to visit the park and run errands. I just need a small break. Let me know..." Response, silence, then a text back saying, "Okay, I'll look at my schedule and let you know.

But nothing ever came of it. While I was disappointed at times when my desire was for certain friends and family to show up, and they chose not to, it was devastating to me. Despite this, I kept myself open to the possibility of a village showing up for us.

I'll walk you through:

- **How I overcame my resistance to asking:** I started small. I asked a friend to pick up groceries. I told a family member I needed an hour to myself. I reminded myself that asking didn't mean I was weak—it meant I was wise enough to preserve my energy.

- **How to identify people you can trust:** I looked for those who had shown up consistently in other seasons. Not just those who said, "Let me know if you need anything," but also those who already knew how to show love in action.

- **Scripts and language to make it easier to reach out:** I learned to say things like, "I'm not okay today—could you check in later?" Or "I don't need solutions, just someone to listen."

- **How to respond when help doesn't come:** I stopped internalizing silence as rejection. I realized not everyone has the capacity, and that's okay. I created backup plans. I widened my circle. I became gentler with my expectations.

- I healed my trauma responses from abandonment early on in life. Because saying "I need help" isn't just about receiving—it's about choosing yourself, again and again.

Practical Tools
That Helped Me Reconnect with Myself:

- Practiced saying "I need help" in the mirror until it felt less heavy.
- Wrote a list titled: "If someone asked how to support me, I'd say…"
- Texted one trusted friend a week, even just to say "Hey, I need to talk."
- Started small, accepting offers to take out the trash or sit with my mom.
- Created reminders on my phone:"It's not weak to receive—it's wise."

Affirmations

○ Asking for help is an act of strength.

○ I don't have to carry it all alone.

○ My needs are valid and worthy of care.

○ Vulnerability builds a deeper connection.

Journal Prompts

1. What makes it hard for me to ask for help?

_____

_____

_____

_____

2. Who in my life has shown up for me without needing to be asked?

_____

_____

_____

_____

3. What is one thing I can delegate this week?

_____

_____

_____

Strength doesn't mean self-sacrifice without support. It means honoring your humanity and giving others the opportunity to love you as well.

MOMENT 5

Building Your Support Circle Without Asking

For most of my life, I have been the strong one. The one people call. The one who figures it out. The one who shows up with a solution, a plan, a comforting word. So when it came time for me to be the one who needed help, I didn't know how.

Asking felt foreign. Vulnerable. Even a little shameful.

Day 21 of being in the hospital I sent a group text sharing how long I had been in the hospital with mom. I shared that since being in there for the holidays, Thanksgiving, and most of December, I had not had a "home cooked" meal. Immediately, the response was "no problem," we will see you on x day at x time. I had food that lasted until we left the hospital to eat on for the next 11 or so days.

There were many times I thought, "If they really loved me, they'd just show up." And honestly? That thought came from past abandonment experiences. I was used to people being people pleasers. People who genuinely cared often didn't need to be asked— they just knew when something was off. They'd pop by with a meal or send a text, even if they heard something in how your voice sounds and would say, "I've got you."

But when caregiving became the center of my world, something shifted. The help I needed wasn't as obvious. It wasn't the kind you could casually check in on. It was deeper. Ongoing. Unspoken. And yet, I still didn't have the language to say, "I need you." High-functioning depression became a reality. Still getting things done, but underneath it all, I cried every single day attempting to release the emotional weight I carried alone.

I allowed the myself to trust the medical team I researched and created. This was imparative and became a huge weight lift as well. This moment is about receiving help without having to ask in traditional ways. About creating a soft place for support to land, even when it's hard to speak it aloud. I'll show you how I created moments:

- **Used gentle honesty to open the door:** I began telling people when I was tired instead of pretending I was fine. I let trusted friends know that I was overwhelmed and didn't have the words but needed presence.

- **Gave people specific ways to help:** I didn't say "I need help" vaguely—I said, "Could you bring a meal on Wednesday?" Or "Would you mind calling to make sure I don't sleep through my alarm?"

- **Learned to accept imperfect offers:** I stopped waiting for help to look perfect. Sometimes people offered support that didn't feel quite right, but I accepted it as a gesture of love.

- **Created a "support menu" so people knew exactly how to plug in:** I made a short list of tasks others could choose from: meal drop-offs, text check-ins, grocery runs, sitting with my loved one for 30 minutes while I walked.

- **Be okay with speaking up and no response:** Don't regress when you speak up and ask for help; no one will answer the call. Continue speaking up and voicing your thoughts and needs.

One of the hardest lessons I had to learn on this journey was allowing myself to receive support.

As caregivers, we're conditioned to believe we must hold everything—every decision, every detail, every fear—on our own. I spent much of my time researching, advocating, and preparing, believing that being strong meant being self-contained.

What I learned instead is that strength sometimes looks like opening your hands and letting others stand beside you.

Over time, I built a care team intentionally—providers I researched, observed, and ultimately chose to walk hand in hand with. Trust wasn't immediate; it was earned, on both sides. I trusted them with the most sacred thing in my life, my mother's care and in return, they learned to trust me. We became a partnership. A team.

One that listens attentively, communicates honestly, and guides one another toward a shared purpose: sustaining her life with dignity, safety, and compassion. There is something deeply grounding about knowing you are not carrying the weight alone, that decisions are made together, and that your voice matters in the room.

Her current primary physician has been a constant anchor through it all. Every step, every concern, every late message or moment of uncertainty she has been there. Not just to manage the medical complexities, but to see me too. She checks on my mother's body, yes but she also pours into my spirit.

She reminds me on what matters, reassures me when the fear creeps in, and affirms the care I give when I quietly question myself. That kind of presence changes everything. It turns appointments into conversations, medicine into humanity, and care into connection.

Practical Tools
That Helped Me Reconnect with Myself:

- Made a simple "support menu" with 3–5 things others could help with.
- Shared weekly check-ins with a friend I trusted, even just via text.
- Realigned receiving help as giving someone else a chance to love me.
- Left subtle cues for support—like saying "Today, I am not ok" out loud.
- Journaled the names of people who have shown up so I wouldn't forget.

Affirmations

- I am not alone, even when I feel isolated.
- I am worthy of help and support.
- Receiving care does not diminish my strength.
- Help can come in unexpected but needed ways.

Journal Prompts

1. What kind of support would you feel good about receiving?

------

2. Who might be open to showing up for me if I gave them guidance?

------

3. What makes it hard for me to receive?

You do not need to do this alone. And you don't have to find the perfect words to be supported. Let others love you in the ways they can.

MOMENT 6

Creating Boundaries in the Midst of Care

Creating boundaries as a caregiver isn't easy. It feels unnatural—almost selfish—when so much of your energy is spent helping someone else survive, heal, or function. But I had to learn, sometimes the hard way, that boundaries are not walls—they're doors. Doors that allow what nourishes me in and keep what depletes me out.

In the beginning, I didn't know how to say no. I felt guilty when I needed time for myself. I feared disappointing others or being judged. But the more I sacrificed my peace, the more resentment I built up—resentment toward the situation, the people around me, and eventually, myself.

Boundaries are the bridge between compassion and sustainability. Without them, caregiving becomes a slow erosion of self. With them, caregiving becomes a shared, sacred rhythm.

In this moment, I walk you through:

- **The signs that you're overdue for boundaries:** When I started snapping at people I loved, crying over small things, or feeling dread at every new ask—I knew I had waited too long. These are signs.

- **Scripts for setting gentle, clear limits:** I practiced saying, "I can't do that right now," or "I'd love to help, but I'm at capacity." Boundaries don't need explanations—just clarity.

- **How to deal with push-back or guilt:** I reminded myself that disappointing someone else was better than betraying myself. I acknowledged the guilt but didn't let it steer me.

What boundaries look like emotionally, physically, spiritually: Emotionally, I stopped absorbing everyone's urgency. Physically, I claimed time to rest. Spiritually, I created rituals—prayer, deep breathing, journaling—to protect my peace.

Practical Tools
That Helped Me Reconnect with Myself:

- Practiced saying "Let me get back to you" as a default response.

- Created a list of my emotional non-negotiable(e.g., no guilt-texts after 8pm).

- Gave myself permission to pause before reacting or agreeing.

- Set silent phone hours of Do Not Disturb.

- Tracked how I felt after saying "yes" or "no" to notice patterns.

- Taking 20 minutes after every appointment just to breathe

Affirmations

- Boundaries protect what matters most.

- I am allowed to take space.

- Saying no creates space for a deeper yes.

- I can be kind and clear at the same time.

Journal Prompts

1. What boundary do I need to protect my peace?

------

2. Where do I feel resentment, and what does it reveal to me?

------

3. How do I know when I've reached my emotional limit?

Boundaries are not a luxury. They are lifelines. And you, dear caregiver, deserve to be held by them.

MOMENT 7

Building a Respite Routine

When you're in the heart of caregiving, the idea of rest can feel impossible. It's not just the physical demands—it's the mental load, the guilt, the planning, the unpredictability. For a long time, I believed respite meant taking a full day or weekend away. And since I couldn't do that, I told myself rest wasn't for me.

But I was wrong.

Respite is not always grand or lengthy. It doesn't have to be booked or scheduled through a service. Respite is any intentional pause that gives your spirit a moment to catch its breath.

The day finally came, it was a Friday, our last day at the nursing/rehab facility. Pure excitement and nervous at the same time. Excited to finally go home and sleep in a bed, but nervous about how things will fare for us. It was just mom and I trying to figure it out. Time to get in the car, and mom is still not walking. There was an aide who became close to us, and she helped me get her in the car. We went to eat at a drive-thru, and now, it's time for me to do it on my own. I was so nervous, not wanting to drop her. I did not have a back brace yet, but I did it. I got her from the car to her wheelchair. From the wheelchair to her recliner, and in that moment, I knew I needed a plan not just for her but myself, too.

This moment is about re-imagining what rest can look like—especially for those of us caring for someone with complex needs, limited mobility, or who are particular about routines.

I learned how to build respite into my day with what I call "rhythmic breathers." These are consistent, manageable breaks that become part of your caregiving rhythm.

Ways I Created a Respite Routine Even in a Full Life

- ꕥ I trained myself to sit down while my loved one napped instead of "catching up" on chores.

- ꕥ I kept a "peace basket" nearby—a small bin with a candle, journal, herbal tea, and a photo of a happy memory.

- ꕥ I used sound—soft music, ocean waves, gospel—to re-center my nervous system in just five minutes.

- ꕥ I found "pocket respite" moments: 3 minutes in the bathroom with the door locked and hand on my chest, breathing. A silent walk to the mailbox. A phone call with a friend while doing laundry.

Actionable Steps to Create Your Routine

1. **Assess Your Current Flow:** What part of your day has even 5 minutes of flexibility?
2. **Choose a Grounding Activity:** Something you can do consistently. Breathing, journaling, stretching.
3. **Stack Your Habit:** Tie your respite moment to an existing action (e.g., every time you warm food, sit with tea).
4. **Set a Timer:** Use reminders if needed. Honor that time as sacred.

Affirmations

- I deserve moments of stillness.

- Rest is not a reward—it is a right.

- Even five minutes of peace can shift my day.

- My well-being matters, too.

Journal Prompts

1. What does rest look like in this season of my life?

------

2. What small moments of pause can I claim today?

------

3. What would I do with 15 uninterrupted minutes?

You don't have to wait for the perfect time or full relief to experience respite. You can create it. You can design it. You can weave it into your day—not just for survival, but for your healing.

MOMENT 8

Self-Care Isn't Selfish: It's Survival

During my period of self-discovery before becoming a full-time caregiver, I learned how to properly care for myself. The things I needed, wanted, and what brought me peace. There was a time when I evolved to all things self-care. I would talk to any and everybody about massages, vacations, or bubble baths, and I'd attempt to encourage them to indulge. I learned so much and immersed myself, even created a brand, InHer Peace, now IHP Beauty (I Have Peace). However, a piece of me went out of the window, and self-care turned into self-preservation for not myself but for the loved one, as I became the advocate.

I was managing medications, juggling schedules, fielding emotional swings, and trying to hold myself together. I gave myself the minimum to show up for someone else. Not good because, as the saying goes, "you are no good for anyone else, if you are not good yourself". As I began to exhale after the long inhale, I felt that I was holding onto self-care and started to return.

I was reminded that self-care isn't just a spa day. It's not luxury—it's maintenance. The tools that I had learned previously were starting to come back to me. It's truly what keeps us from falling apart when everything else is falling apart.

I learned the hard way that ignoring myself didn't make me

more noble. It made me more resentful. More burnt out. More likely to snap at the people I love. The turning point came when I realized: if I collapse, everyone I care for is affected. My health is not a side note. It's foundational.

In this moment, I share how I redefined self-care—not as something extra, but as something essential.

How I Made Self-Care Work Even When Life Was Full

- I gave myself permission to make rest a priority, not a reward.
- I started asking, "What do I need right now?" and listening to the answer.
- I created five-minute rituals that reminded me I existed beyond the caregiver role.

Simple, Sustainable Self-Care Practices

- Drinking water with intention and gratitude.
- Writing down one sentence a day about how I felt.
- Sitting in silence and placing my hand on my heart.
- Saying no to things that felt heavy.
- Saying yes to myself even when it felt unfamiliar.

Affirmations

- I am worthy of care.

- My well-being matters.

- Tending to myself is a radical act of love.

- I give myself permission to rest, to feel, to be.

Journal Prompts

1. What is one thing I can do today to honor myself?

----

2. What makes me feel grounded, safe, or at ease?

----

3. Where have I been putting myself last, and how can I change that?

Self-care is not selfish. It is how we survive. It is how we reclaim ourselves. It is how we make sure we're still here, still who.e, still able to love without losing ourselves in the process. You deserve to be well.

MOMENT 9

Letting Go of Guilt: You Deserve Rest

Guilt has a way of making itself at home in caregiving. I used to feel guilty for taking a nap, for going to the store alone, for laughing too hard when my loved one was having a hard day. Guilt crept into the smallest cracks of joy, whispering, "You should be doing more." I remember the first time I had to leave the house and had no one to sit with my mom. I needed to run errands that I couldn't have had delivered, and even though it wasn't for a long period of time. It was still time away.

I bought cameras for each room so I could check in and talk to her via the camera intercom. But still I felt guilt leaving her alone, thoughts ran through my head like anything could happen, but I had to trust and have faith that while I am physically alone caring for her, I am not alone spiritually, and she is covered.

But guilt is not a compass—it's a weight. And if we don't confront, the weight will anchor us in a place where rest feels like betrayal and joy feels unearned. The gentle reminder that we as caregivers are no good to your loved one or person you are caring for if you are not good to yourself.

In this moment, I explore what guilt looks like in real caregiving moments:

I used to think guilt was proof that I cared. But now I know better. Love and guilt are not the same. True love invites rest. True care includes the caregiver.

Practical Tools
That Helped Me Reconnect with Myself:

- Wrote out "guilt vs. truth" statements to challenge toxic thoughts.

- Practiced saying, "Resting is not abandoning, resting is replenishing."

- Took 5 minutes of quiet time after doing anything for someone else.

- Made a visual list of small joys I denied myself—and started claiming them.

- Talked to my guilt as if it were a child: "I see you. I hear you. But I choose grace."

How I Work Through Guilt

- I name it: "This is guilt, not truth."

- I write down what I'm afraid it means (e.g., "If I rest, I'm selfish").

- 🕊 I speak to myself as I would to a friend: "You deserve to breathe."
- 🕊 I choose one small act of kindness toward myself—on purpose.
- 🕊 When I left the room to catch my breath, my loved one called out.
- 🕊 When I laughed at a movie while they rested in pain.
- 🕊 When I said "no" to a visit because I had nothing left to give.

Affirmations

- Guilt does not define my love.

- I am allowed to enjoy my life while caring for someone else.

- Rest is not selfish. It's sacred.

- I honor my limits without shame.

Journal Prompts

1. Where do I feel guilty in my caregiving role?

------

2. What would I say to a friend carrying this same guilt?

------

3. What truth do I want to hold onto when guilt shows up?

Letting go of guilt is not a one-time act—it's a practice. But every time you release it, even a little, you make space for something gentler: grace.

You deserve grace. You deserve peace. You deserve to rest—without apology.

MOMENT 10

Finding Your Joy Again

There was a time when I could hop on a plane at a moment's notice. When I filled my passport with stamps, danced barefoot on foreign sand, and journaled beside quiet lakes. Back then, freedom was my joy. Movement was my medicine.

But then caregiving came. Not abruptly, but in waves. And slowly, the spontaneity faded. The bags stayed unpacked. The calendar is filled with doctor visits instead of departure dates. And I began to wonder: Would I ever feel like myself again?

The answer is yes—but not in the same way. I had to find a new kind of joy. One that didn't rely on escape, but instead invited me to be fully present, even here.

As a single Black woman in her 40s, with no husband nor children, I thought I had all the freedom in the world. And in some ways, I did. But when the needs of my loved one became central, I felt my identity begin to slip. I was no longer the woman who traveled, who dreamed freely. I was the one who stayed. Who cared. Who held it all together.

The moment came when I began to shift back to myself. I was living at the nursing/rehab facility with my mom and got a random text from a friend. "Dinner at 8p? I responded without hesitation. I can do 8:30p. It was almost as if I had an immediate response without thinking to consider my current situation. I got dressed in the bathroom of her patient care room, called a ride, and off I went. I found my way back within two hours before meds were passed, but it was the most normalcy I had in a very long time.

And yet—joy remained inside me. Dormant, but not dead. So, I

began to seek it in small ways:

Where I Found Joy Again - Practical Tools That Helped Me Reconnect with Myself:

- In sunlight through my window while washing dishes.
- In dancing to old-school R&B while folding laundry.
- In reading stories that made me feel seen.
- In writing letters to my future self, reminding her I hadn't forgotten her.

Joy became something I created, not something I waited for.

Practical Tools
That Helped Me Reconnect with Myself

- Made a "joy inventory" of past and present things that lit me up.
- Created a weekly joy ritual—coffee, dancing, or journaling to music.
- Took 1 photo a week of something that made me smile—no matter how small.
- Sent a kind letter or text to my future self saying: "You didn't forget you."

How I Rebuilt a Joy Practice

1. I wrote down 5 things that used to bring me joy.
2. I circled the ones that were still accessible in some form.
3. I committed to one joy-filled action a week—even if it was for five minutes.
4. I shared these moments with a friend, to help me stay accountable to my own delight.

Affirmations

○ My joy is still mine to claim.

○ I am allowed to feel light, even when life is heavy.

○ Joy is not betrayal—it's a return.

○ I can laugh without apology.

Journal Prompts

1. What used to make me feel alive?

---

2. What's one small thing that brings a smile to my face today?

---

3. How can I create a moment of joy this week?

You haven't lost yourself—you've been carrying pieces of yourself all along. Let this moment be your permission to pick them back up. To feel joy again. To come home to yourself.

Because even in caregiving, even in stillness, even in grief joy is not only possible. It's necessary.

MOMENT 11

Building a Sustainable Life Beyond the Crisis

There comes a moment—sometimes quietly, sometimes in exhaustion—when you realize you can't keep doing things the same way. You've been living in survival mode so long that you forgot what normal even felt like. But survival is not the same as living. It keeps you breathing, but it doesn't let you thrive. Somewhere deep inside, a soft truth begins to whisper that it doesn't have to be this hard forever.

I reached that place after another all-night living in the rehab, nursing facility. I was tired in my bones. And it wasn't just physical—it was emotional, mental, spiritual depletion. I realized the rhythm I created wasn't sustainable. And if I wanted to live, not just function, I needed to rebuild.

This moment is about moving beyond the urgent into the intentional. It's about creating a rhythm that honors your life, your dreams, your well-being—even while caregiving continues. Because you can lose yourself in the chaos, or you can choose to find yourself again in the stillness between. That's where I learned that rebuilding isn't just about survival—it's about giving yourself permission to live with hope, with joy, with grace, even in the middle of the hard.

My Steps Toward Sustainability

- 𝛾 I simplified routines and let go of perfection.
- 𝛾 I scheduled rest as seriously as appointments.
- 𝛾 I delegated where possible, even if it felt uncomfortable.
- 𝛾 I said no more often, without long explanations.

Tools That Helped Me Shift

- 𝛾 A whiteboard for weekly planning and margin.
- 𝛾 A journal check-in every Sunday: What worked? What didn't?
- 𝛾 A meal service for at least one day a week.
- 𝛾 A quiet corner of my home that's just for me.

Sustainability Means...

- 𝛾 You eat before you're starving.
- 𝛾 You sleep without guilt.
- 𝛾 You build joy into your life before burnout forces you to.

Affirmations

- I am allowed to redesign my life.

- I deserve rhythms that restore me.

- My life is worth living fully—not just surviving.

- I can care for others and still honor myself.

Journal Prompts

1. What's one thing I do out of obligation that I could release?

------

2. Where can I invite more ease into my life?

------

3. What would a sustainable week look like?

We can build lives that nourish us—not just for the crisis, but for the long road ahead. It starts with one small change. One new choice. One deep breath that says, "I'm rebuilding—for me."

MOMENT 12

When You're Ready to Let Go

Letting go doesn't always mean walking away. Sometimes, it means loosening your grip on how you thought things had to be. It means grieving the version of life you imagined and embracing the one that is unfolding before you. I was ready to let go of control.

We cannot control all things, and that was the grip I held onto. If I am honest, I still work daily to intentionally release, regardless of what is happening around me.

The exact moment I knew I was ready to let go came during a disagreement with my mom over what she wanted to eat. I had been doing everything I could to help manage her rising blood pressure—lemon water with Ceylon cinnamon, beet juice, hibiscus tea. I'd researched endlessly, poured myself into finding natural ways to support her healing. But she just wanted chips and dip. Popcorn. Fried food from restaurants. She'd have a good streak, and then one choice would unravel everything we'd worked so hard to stabilize.

That day, in the middle of our argument, she looked at me and said, "You're trying to control my life. The only time I have peace is when I'm asleep."

Her words hit like a punch to the chest.

I'd been so focused on her healing that I forgot just how far we'd come. Less than six months earlier, I was praying she would eat at all. Now, I was hoping she'd make better choices—not just for her, but for me, because I am her sole caregiver. But in that moment, I realized I needed to support her, not control her. It is her life, not mine.

I had to let go of my attachment to her, making the "right" choices. What I was really trying to do was protect the little girl inside me who had never stopped being afraid of losing her mom. The girl who remembered being 14 years old and hearing the words, "She may not live past four more years."

That trauma, that fear—I needed to release it.

Letting go of that fear doesn't mean giving up. It means choosing to live in the present. It means finding peace in the fact that I get to love and enjoy my mom today, just as she is.

As caregivers, we carry so much—hope, fear, plans, guilt, exhaustion, love. We hold onto routines, roles, and responsibilities with clenched fists because we think if we loosen up, something will break. But often, it's the clenching that is breaking us. It turns into codependency with your loved one and you being the caregiver, "no one can take care of my loved one like me," or "there won't be any errors if I do it". Being her protector is my responsibility, a role I have also assumed.

I had to learn this slowly, painfully. Letting go didn't mean I loved my mom any less. It meant I started loving myself, too. Letting go meant releasing:

- The idea that I could fix everything
- The belief that if I were strong enough, she wouldn't decline
- The image of perfection I had in my mind

Letting go meant surrendering to what was real and loving fully from that space.

When I Knew I Was Ready to Let Go

- I stopped re-explaining her condition to people who didn't want to understand
- I stepped back from relationships that only took but never gave back in
- I cried without rushing to clean up my face.
- I forgave myself for not being everything to everyone.

This moment walks you through the sacred and painful practice of releasing—bit by bit.

Steps Toward Letting Go

1. Name what you're holding on to.
2. Ask what it's costing you.
3. Choose one thing to release today.
4. Create a letting-go ritual (such as writing a letter, taking a walk, or performing a symbolic action).

Affirmations

- Letting go is not giving up—it is choosing peace.

- I can love and let go at the same time.

- I release the need to control what is not mine to carry.

- My worth is not tied to how tightly I hold on.

Journal Prompts

1. What am I still holding on to that no longer serves me?

---

2. What would letting go feel like in my body?

---

3. Who am I when I release the weight of perfection?

This moment is not about abandonment—it's about alignment. It's about making room for healing, clarity, and breath. You are allowed to let go of what is breaking you so you can receive what is building you.

MOMENT 13

Grief, Growth, and Grace

Grief is not linear. It doesn't politely knock and wait its turn. It barges in, unannounced—sometimes years after a loss, sometimes in the middle of laughter. As a caregiver, I didn't know I was grieving while I was still in the middle of it all.

I grieved the way things used to be. I grieved the freedom I had before the diagnoses and hospital visits. I grieved the ease of simple days, of spontaneous choices. But I also grieved silently—the kind of grief that hides behind being strong.

And yet, I grew.

Growth didn't come with fanfare. It came with silent revelations. It came with the ability to hold two things at once: pain and gratitude, anger and love, sorrow, and hope. This moment explores the dance of grief and growth and the grace that made space for both.

And still, there is the grief no one talks about—the grief that comes from realizing the people you thought would stand beside you, didn't. The silence from those you once showed up for echoes louder when you're at your lowest. I had to grieve the loss of expectation. I had to forgive—not always for their sake, but for mine.

Forgiveness isn't always a grand moment. Sometimes it's just whispering to yourself, *"they couldn't show up for me, but I will not carry this weight another day"*. And that's grace, too.

Grief didn't ask for my permission. But growth? Growth required my participation. And grace—it met me in the cracks. Not the polished places, but the broken, tired, messy middle where I learned to be soft with myself. Where I learned that showing up was enough for me.

This part of the journey is where I stop waiting to be rescued and start honoring the strength it took to survive without the rescue. Where I make peace with the pain, hold space for the process, and keep walking—with grief in one hand and grace in the other.

Where Grief Showed Up Unexpectedly

- Hearing an old song that reminded me of simpler times
- Watching someone else live freely while I stayed back
- Seeing my loved one change and knowing they'd never be the same

How I Held Grief and Still Chose Growth

- I named my grief. Out loud. In writing. In prayer.
- I let myself feel without explaining it to anyone.
- I began to honor small wins as real progress.
- I forgave myself for needing more than I thought I should.

Grace Made Room For Me To...

- Rest when I felt guilty.
- Love without having all the answers.
- Start again after shutting down.
- Speak my truth even when it was messy.

Affirmations

- I am allowed to grieve what was and grow into what's next.

- I trust that healing is not always visible.

- My story is still being written—with grace.

- Grief is not a weakness. It is love with nowhere to go.

Journal Prompts

1. What am I still grieving?

---

2. What growth have I seen in myself that I haven't acknowledged?

---

3. Where do I need grace right now?

Grief, growth, and grace aren't separate—they often travel together. You can cry and rise. You can break and become. And you can love yourself through every part of it.

You don't have to rush your healing. Just take the next breath. That, too, is grace.

MOMENT 14

Reflections from Other Caregivers

Caregiver is not a one-size-fits-all journey. While the emotional weight may be familiar, the stories, dynamics, and lessons vary widely. This moment holds space for the reflections of others who have walked this path.

Each voice brings something sacred—insight, validation, hope. These caregivers allowed their experiences to be shared so that you, the reader, feel less alone. Whether you're just starting or have been in this role for years, may these stories bring comfort, courage, and connection.

Reflection from Bryce, 45 — Caring for his aging parents, both diagnosed with stage 4 cancer

"My caregiving journey is deeply rooted in my love for my parents. Since childhood, I've always been close to them, especially my mother, who has struggled with heart disease throughout my life. For decades, despite multiple heart surgeries, life continued steadily for our family – until November 5, 2023.

Caring for someone with cancer involves far more than physical tasks; it requires emotional strength, patience, and the ability to remain calm and reassuring. My days became consumed with hospital visits and managing his treatment schedule. As the cancer progressed to his legs, he lost all mobility in his lower body, and my responsibilities expanded to feeding, lifting, cleaning, and changing him daily.

These days were and still are long, and the nights felt even longer. I often doubted whether I could keep going, as the mental and emotional toll was unlike anything I had ever experienced. Yet I remained deeply grateful for the support of my family and friends. On March 19th, 2024, my father passed away peacefully at home.

Shortly after, my focus shifted to caring for my mother, who has now been diagnosed with stage four cancer herself. My story as a caregiver is still unfolding. Entering this journey with no prior experience, I've learned so much about myself – about resilience, adaptability, and the true meaning of compassion.

Through this experience, I have come to understand that when a person is sick, illness doesn't just happen to them; it happens to the entire family. Effective caregiving requires understanding a loved one's physical and emotional needs, maintaining clear and gentle communication, and prioritizing self-care to prevent burnout. Patience, adaptability, time management, and organization have become essential skills for me."

Reflection from Tanya, 52 — Caring for a spouse with early-onset Alzheimer's

"At first, I didn't want to admit how scared I was. My husband forgetting where we lived was the first sign. He had always been so sharp. I cried in the pantry that night because I didn't want him to see me fall apart. Now I celebrate every small moment of connection. I've learned to find joy in glances, in touch, and in the sacredness of showing up daily—even when he doesn't remember who I am."

Reflection from Malik, 34 — Caring for his aging grandfather

"Being a Black man in a caregiver role isn't talked about enough. People assume we don't feel the emotional toll. But I grieve in silence sometimes. I carry the legacy of my grandfather, and caring for him feels like honoring that. Still, I had to learn to set boundaries, even with family, so I didn't lose myself. Therapy helped me stay grounded."

Reflection from Anita, 47 — Caring for a medically fragile child

"People call me a supermom, but I'm just a mother trying to survive. There were times I didn't sleep for 48 hours. I've lived in and out of hospitals, memorized medications, and learned to advocate with a voice I didn't know I had. What saved me was the community—finding other parents who understood. We text each other through the darkest nights. That's what keeps me going."

Reflection from Jerome, 59 — Caring for his sister with a disability

"My sister has been my responsibility since our parents passed. I gave up a promotion because she needed me. Some days I'm proud. Some days I'm bitter. Most days, I'm tired. But she has also taught me patience, tenderness, and what unconditional love truly looks like. I still dream for myself—and that's okay."

Dear Caregiver, Thank you.

Wow, what a ride this has been. Thank you for taking this journey with me. Thank you for being brave enough to pause, to reflect, and to reclaim pieces of yourself along the way. Your vulnerability and ability to surrender in order to choose you is liberating. Whether you read this guide in quiet moments between responsibilities or devoured it during a time of transformation, I hope it reminded you of one powerful truth:

You are still here. And you are still you.

This book wasn't written to tell you what to do—it was written to hold your hand as you remember how much you've already done. It was written to create space for your tired heart, your full schedule, your complicated emotions, and your sacred humanity.

Caregiving is an act of deep love—but so is caring for yourself. You are allowed to rest. You are allowed to feel. You are allowed to take up space in your own life.

My prayer is that you come back to these pages whenever you need comfort, perspective, or permission to choose yourself again. And again. And again.

You are not invisible. You are not alone.

You are not lost.

You are seen. You are valued. You are enough. With so much love,

Shellie Stark

MOMENT 15

Journal Section: Your Space to Be Seen

This is your moment. Not mine. Not anyone else's. Yours. This is where you don't have to explain, perform, or filter your truth. This is where your story, your exhaustion, your joy, and your questions are allowed to breathe on the page.

You've carried so much, often silently. Let this be the space that listens back.

Your Story Belongs Here

This moment is also a living invitation. If you're reading this and thinking, "My story could help someone," know that there's space for you, too.

Use the pages that follow to write your own reflection.

1. What have you learned?

----

2. What would you tell someone just starting the journey?

----

3. How has caregiving changed you?

You are not alone. And your voice matters.

Journal Prompts

1. What does caregiving look like in my world?

----

2. How has this experience changed me—for better and for harder?

----

3. What do I miss about the version of me before caregiving?

---

4. When was the last time I felt seen?

---

5. What do I need today—and what have I been too afraid to ask for?

Affirmation Space:
Write your own. Speak it daily. Let it root you in your truth.

- Today, I am *giving myself grace* .

- I allow myself to *take a 20-minute break* .

- I am worthy of *rest*.

- Even when *I feel behind, I still believe I am right where I am supposed to be.*

A Letter to Yourself: Write a letter to:

- Your current self
- Your future self
- The version of you that started this journey

Tell her/him what you wish they knew. Tell them what you're proud of. Tell them they have never been forgotten. I'll go first and share my letters that I have written to myself and to others. Rather it was someone I have been truly grateful for and someone who truly disappointed me during this caregiver journey.

My Letters to Myself:

Dear Shellie,

I see you. I see the way your body has learned to sleep sitting up in hospital chairs. I see how your hair turned completely gray from nights spent listening to machines beep, from holding your mom's hand when she couldn't speak, from crying quietly in public restrooms so no one would hear you break.

You've been living in battle mode for months now—1 ½ months in this hospital room, and now another 2 ½ months journey in this nursing home that feels more like a revolving door than a place of healing. You've advocated harder than anyone should ever have to. You've seen too much. You've watched as care became neglect, as compassion turned cold, and you had no choice but to step in—again and again—because if you didn't, who would?

You've begged God for strength on bathroom floors. You've whispered prayers through clenched teeth while wiping your mother's face. And you've smiled through pain that could've swallowed you whole. You fought with supernatural strength. You became her voice. Her shield. Her everything.

But, my love, I also know what you were carrying silently. You were lonely. Devastatingly so.

Family didn't show up the way you hoped they would. Friends you thought would reach out didn't. No one asked how you were really doing. And when they did, you smiled because you didn't have the words to say, "I'm drowning." And when you did, it fell on deaf ears as though you never said it.

I want to tell you—it wasn't weakness that made you feel that way. It was the truth. You deserved help. You deserved someone to hold your hand, make you tea, sit with you, and say, "You don't have to do this alone." I'm sorry, no one consistently did that.

But oh, how you kept showing up anyway.

Your faith kept you grounded when the system failed you. Your inner voice became your compass when the noise around you got too loud. You trusted your instincts. You trusted your discernment. And when no one else could, you learned to hold yourself.

I am so proud of you for that.

You didn't imagine the injustice. You didn't overreact. You carried the weight of love, loss, rage, and responsibility with grace, even when it didn't feel graceful. You did not fail your mother. You saved her time and time again.

I want you to know this: what you endured was not fair, but it was formative. It cracked you open in ways that revealed your truest self—not the one always smiling, but the one fiercely rooted in truth, love, and sacred fire.

And though you felt alone, you were never abandoned. Your ancestors, your Creator, your inner knowing—they carried you when your legs couldn't. You are not broken. You are holy. You are the living proof that love, real love, knows no limits.

So, take this moment now, and breathe. Not just for her—but for you. You don't have to carry it all anymore.

You are allowed to exhale. You are allowed to be held.

And you are so deeply, beautifully loved. With compassion and truth.

XO ~ Me

Dear Me, Look at you.

Look at the way you breathe deeper now. The way your shoulders sit lower, softer—not from surrendering to stress, but from releasing what was never yours to carry. Look at the glow in your eyes—not one that came from ease, but from rising through the fire and choosing yourself anyway.

You've come so far girlie.

You fought long and hard through survival seasons that most people will never understand. But now you've started to heal. You gave yourself permission to rest. To feel. To begin again— not as the person people expected you to be, but as the woman you were always becoming.

Therapy gave you language for the ache. It helped untangle the guilt, the rage, the exhaustion, the loneliness—and the love. You let your words unfold without apology. You didn't edit your truth to make others more comfortable. You spoke it clearly, kindly, and without shrinking. That alone is a revolution.

When you look in the mirror now, you see yourself. Not just the caregiver. Not just the warrior. But the full, beautiful soul behind it all. You see the softness that survived. The laughter is coming back. The quiet confidence rooted in truth, not performance.

You're rooted now—in your worth, in your peace, in your knowing.

You no longer abandon yourself for the comfort of others. You've learned the art of saying now without guilt. You've set boundaries that hold your energy sacred, even with the people you love the most. Especially with them. Because you understand now:

boundaries aren't rejection—they're remembrance. Of who you are. Of what matters.

You walk daily now—not just for exercise, but for clarity. For grounding. For joy. You let the breeze remind you of God's presence, of your breath, of your becoming. Those walks are your moving prayers.

You cook meals that comfort you—not just out of necessity, but out of delight. You hum while stirring. You dance barefoot in the kitchen. You eat slowly, not rushed. You enjoy your own company. You remember what it feels like to be alive, not just functioning.

You are the living proof of what happens when a woman chooses herself with love. I hope you keep choosing her.

She's worth it.

With love, reverence, and pride,

XO ~ Me

A Letter from You to Someone Else (Optional)

Who needs to hear your truth? Who needs to hear your gratitude? Who needs to hear your boundaries? Who needs to hear that you're healing?

Write it. You don't have to send it. Let it be medicine for your own release. I'll share my letters with you.

A Letter of Gratitude

Dear Genuine Friend,

I want to thank you—not just in passing, not just with a simple "I appreciate you," but with the fullness of my heart. There are no words big enough to capture what your presence has meant to me, but I'll try, because you deserve to know.

You never met my mother. You never stepped into her hospital room or walked through the doors of that nursing facility. But you were there. Night after night. Call after call. Listening to symptoms, reading through medical charts, helping me connect the dots when I could barely keep my head above water.

You didn't come with big promises or dramatic declarations. You came with consistency. With grace. With a quiet, unwavering strength. And you never made it about you—even when it could have been. You never asked me to shrink my pain so you could feel more comfortable. Instead, you held the space. You sat in it with me. You honored the weight without trying to fix it.

There's something sacred about being seen in your unraveling and not judged for it. There were days I didn't have words, just sighs. And you still stayed on the phone.

There were times I questioned everything—and you didn't rush to give me answers. You just reminded me I wasn't alone in figuring it out.

What humbles me the most is this: you showed up for me while carrying your own story of grief. You've lost both of your parents. You've known the ache that never quite leaves. And still—you found a piece within yourself to show up for me. You reached into your own wounds and extended your hand. That kind of love is deep. That kind of empathy is earned. That kind of support is sacred.

You gave me a soft place to land in a season that felt anything but soft. And for that—I will never forget you.

Thank you for every late night, every note you helped me read through, every ounce of energy you poured in without needing acknowledgment. Thank you for being selfless and steady. Thank you for never asking me to perform strength when I was falling apart.

You were—and are—a lifeline.

With love, humility, and deep gratitude,

XO ~ Shellie

A Letter I Never Thought I'd Have to Write

Dear You,

This isn't the letter I wanted to write. It's not the letter I imagined when I pictured this season of my life—or our relationship.

In my heart, I believed without question that you would be there. That your presence wouldn't need to be requested, reminded, or begged for. That you would just know—the way I have shown up for you. The way my mother has sacrificed, supported, and loved without hesitation.

But what happened cut deep.

You chose to do the bare minimum. Or nothing at all. And I don't say that from a place of perfection, but from a place of pain. Because while I was in the trenches—fighting for my mother's life, carrying the weight of decisions, paperwork, sleepless nights, and silent fears—I kept looking for your face in the crowd.

You weren't there.

And what followed were emotions that crashed in waves: disbelief, resentment, anger, sadness, disappointment. A grief that went beyond the medical crises. A grieving of the relationship I thought we had. The bond I thought we built.

I've replayed conversations. Rewritten expectations. Tried to explain it away to protect my heart. But the truth is—it hurt. And it still does.

You had a choice. And I understand—we all do. You chose distance. You chose silence. You chose absence. And while I honor your

free will, I can't deny how it left me: carrying more than I could handle, wondering why the village I gave my all to didn't return the same.

I've learned that ships are meant to carry us when we're too weary to carry ourselves. Friendships. Family-ships. But when the ship tips and no one throws a life jacket, it feels like drowning.

I'm no longer asking why. I'm setting boundaries—with you, and with myself. I've learned that my peace matters. That I deserve reciprocal love, not obligation. That I don't have to stay emotionally tethered to someone who showed me—clearly—that they wouldn't row when I was sinking.

Still, my prayer is this: That this moment does not harden my heart. That it teaches me—not just how to grieve, but how to guard my spirit. That I remain open to divine connection with a like-minded village. People who don't just say they care, but show it. People who know how to carry and be carried.

From now on, I will put my life jacket on first. I am responsible for saving myself—so I can keep living, not just surviving.

And while I'm stepping away from what was, I do so with grace, not bitterness. I choose freedom. I choose truth. And I choose to surround myself with people who show they care—not just when it's convenient.

Good bye doesn't always mean anger. Sometimes it means release. With both ache and clarity,

XO ~ Shellie

A Letter of Love

Dear Consistent Soul,

I don't even know where to begin, because 'thank you' just doesn't seem like enough. But I need to try. From the moment everything shifted after my mom's stroke, you've been there—really there—in a way that only someone with a heart like yours could be.

I've watched you balance your own life, your own responsibilities, your own quiet struggles, and still you chose to show up. Not just in the early days at the hospital when everything felt raw and uncertain, but long after, too—when the routines got heavy, when the emotions settled into our bones, when most people naturally drift away. You didn't. You kept your word. You stayed present. And that consistency? That love? It has held me together more times than I can count.

You weren't obligated. You didn't have to step in the way you did. But you did—And every time, I felt seen. I felt supported. I felt like I wasn't doing this alone.

It has been a journey—one with moments that have broken me and remade me. But having you beside me has brought light into the hardest of days. You are more than family—you are the kind of soul people pray for when they ask for someone to help them carry the weight.

Your bond with Mom is something sacred. I've seen the way her face softens when she hears your voice, how she lights up in your presence, how safe she feels when you're near. You don't

just care for her—you see her. You remind her, and me, that she's still deeply loved and never alone.

It has been a journey—one with moments that have broken me and remade me. But having you beside me has brought light into the hardest of days. You are more than family—you are the kind of soul people pray for when they ask for someone to help them carry the weight.

I hope you know how deeply I appreciate you. Not just for what you've done, but for who you are. Your loyalty, your compassion, your quiet strength—it's changed me. It's lifted me. And I will never forget it.

With all my love and more gratitude than words could ever hold.

XO ~ Shellie

A Letter of Gratitude to the Physician Who Saw Us Human First

I want to take a moment to express a gratitude that words will never fully capture, but I hope you feel it in every line of this letter.

You entered our lives during one of the most fragile and heartbreaking seasons—after the stroke, after the fear had already settled in, when everything felt uncertain and heavy. From the very beginning, you did more than assume the role of a primary care physician. You honored it. You showed up with excellence, attentiveness, and something far more rare: humanity.

Because of the way you care—because you listen, because you respond, because you see my mother as a person and not just a chart—I get to spend more time with her. That is a gift beyond measure. Time is sacred, and your diligence, discernment, and follow-through have protected it. You have helped preserve not just her health, but our moments, our conversations, our laughter, our continued life together.

What has meant just as much to me is how you have poured into me as her caregiver. You have never dismissed my concerns or made me feel invisible in the process. Instead, you've treated me as a partner, a voice at the table, someone whose observations and intuition matter. In moments when I felt overwhelmed or unsure, your calm presence and steady guidance grounded me. You reminded me that I wasn't walking this path alone.

You practice medicine with skill, yes—but more importantly, you lead with compassion. You see the human first. That is rare. And it is healing in ways no prescription could ever replicate.

Thank you for your integrity. Thank you for your patience. Thank you for your care—of my mother, and of me. Our lives are better, fuller, and steadier because of you. I will always carry deep gratitude for the way you showed up when it mattered most.

XO ~ Shellie

To the Physician Who Held Me When I Was Breaking

This letter lives here because you lived in one of the most tender chapters of my life.

You met me at my lowest point—when everything happened at once, when the ground beneath me shifted, when strength felt like something I used to know but could no longer reach. In that moment, you did not rush me. You did not judge me. You did not reduce me to symptoms or silence my pain with clinical distance. You saw me.

You supported my mental health in a way that went far beyond medicine. You held space when I was breaking. You held my hand energetically, intuitively knowing how to show up for me when words were hard to find. You met me where I was, not where I was "supposed" to be. And in doing so, you reminded me that care can be gentle, that healing does not require me to be composed, and that it is okay to fall apart in the presence of someone safe.

What mattered just as much was how you saw me. You didn't just see a patient—you saw a woman. A Black woman. A daughter who loved her mother deeply and was fighting to hold everything together while quietly unraveling inside. You honored my humanity, my grief, my devotion, and my exhaustion. You understood the weight I was carrying without asking me to justify it.

In moments when the world felt dim and narrow, you reminded me there was still a rainbow—that it does get better. Not in a dismissive way, but in a grounded, steady way that allowed hope to feel believable again. You offered reassurance without erasing my reality. You gave me something I didn't know I needed at the time: permission to keep going. Your medical wisdom mattered. Your professionalism mattered. But what changed me was your presence.

This book exists, in part, because of the care you gave me when I couldn't give it to myself. Because you chose compassion. Because you saw me whole. I carry deep gratitude for you—not just as my physician, but as a witness to my survival.

Thank you for holding me in that season.

Thank you for reminding me that light returns.

Thank you for seeing Still Me, even when I couldn't see her yet.

XO ~ Shellie

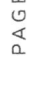

(Use the space on the following pages to write freely. No prompt necessary. Just you, your pen, and your presence.)

Date:

Thoughts:

Date:

Emotions I'm holding today:

Date:

What I wish someone would say to me right now:

This is your space. Let it be soft. Let it be honest. Let it hold you.

You are allowed to be fully seen—by others, but most importantly, by yourself.

MOMENT 16

Resource Toolkit

This moment is your lifeline—a collection of tools, organizations, ideas, and daily practices that have helped me navigate the caregiver journey. I created this section for you to return to any time you need grounding, guidance, or a starting point when everything feels overwhelming.

Emergency Reset Tools: When everything feels like too much, start here:

- 4-7-8 Breathing: Inhale for 4, hold for 7, exhale for 8. Repeat 4x.

- Hand on heart: Close your eyes, breathe, and whisper, "I am safe. I am here."

- Sit by a window: Let the sun hit your skin. Drink water. Say nothing.

Daily Rhythms for the Overwhelmed Caregiver

- Morning mantra: "Today, I will meet myself with compassion."

- Midday check-in: One sentence journal entry (How am I really?)

- Nighttime wind-down: Herbal tea, no screens 30 minutes before bed, quiet music.

Support Organizations

(Please research and select resources specific to your location and needs.)

- Family Caregiver Alliance (caregiver.org)
- AARP Caregiving Resources
- The National Alliance for Caregiving
- Local faith-based or nonprofit caregiver respite programs
- Paid Carevier Programs - Search for State Programs

Mental Health Support

(Please do your own research and choose based on your need, as these are only suggestions)

- Therapy for Black Girls (therapyforblackgirls.com)
- Betterhelp (Betterhelp.com)
- Grow Therapy (Growtherapy.com)
- Talkspace (Talkspace.com)
- Headway (Headway.co)
- Open Path Collective (low-cost therapy: penpathcollective.org)
- Mental Health America screening tools (mhanational.org)

Books That Held Me Together

- "The Art of Extreme Self-Care" by Cheryl Richardson
- "Set Boundaries, Find Peace" by Nedra Glover Tawwab
- "When Things Fall Apart" by Pema Chödrön
- "Rest Is Resistance" by Tricia Hersey

Apps That Help Me Pause

- Insight Timer (guided meditations, affirmations)
- Calm or YouTube meditations (stress & sleep support)
- Trello (to organize appointments, meds, and schedules)
- YouTube and Podcast – Seen & Supported with Shellie Stark

Questions to Ask Medical Teams

1. What's the realistic expectation for the next 6 months?
2. What can I do less of to avoid burnout?
3. Is palliative care an option even without a terminal diagnosis?
4. Are there free or sliding-scale services available?

Preparing for Help

- 🕊 Create a Care Binder: Include medication lists, doctors' information, emergency contacts, and daily routines.
- 🕊 Build a "Respite Contact List": Who can sit with your loved one for 1 hour? Who can run errands?
- 🕊 Write 3 sample text messages asking for help so you're ready when you need them.

Spiritual Grounding

- 🕊 Write a breath prayer: Inhale "I receive," exhale "what I need."
- 🕊 Keep a short scripture, mantra, or quote nearby.
- 🕊 Create a Sabbath moment weekly: Even 10 minutes where you do nothing.

This toolkit is not about doing more—it's about making things lighter.

Come back to this when you need to. Print it. Post it. Share it.

You deserve to have tools that serve you, not just those you care for. You matter here, too.

BONUS SECTION

Caregiver Tools & Templates

Week of

Top 3 Priorities

1.
2.
3.

Appointments + Important Dates

DAY	APPOINTMENT / TASK	TIME	NOTES
MONDAY			
TUESDAY			
THURSDAY			
FRIDAY			
SATURDAY			
SUNDAY			

Use this section as a guide for your personal journal to write down the below:

*Do not over think it. Start out with at least three people and go from there.

Who Is In Your Support Circle?

LIST NAMES	AND TASKS / CHECK-IN	CONTACT INFO	CONTACT INFO

Personal Care Goals

MENTAL

A PHYSICAL

SPIRITUAL

EMOTIONAL

Weekly Anchor Word:

Weekly Reflection: What do I want to feel by the end of this week?

Daily Affirmation

Every breath I take is a return to myself.

What's On My Heart Today?

Daily Affirmation

I honor the strength it takes to show up—every single day.

What's On My Heart Today?

Daily Affirmation

Even in the chaos, I am worthy of peace.

What's On My Heart Today?

Daily Affirmation

My needs matter just as much as the person I care for.

What's On My Heart Today?

Daily Affirmation

○ I release guilt and give myself permission to rest.

What's On My Heart Today?

Daily Affirmation

○ It is okay to not have all the answers. I can ask for help.

What's On My Heart Today?

Daily Affirmation

Today, I choose to be gentle with myself.

What's On My Heart Today?

Daily Affirmation

I am more than my role—I am a whole person with dreams.

What's On My Heart Today?

Daily Affirmation

I deserve moments of joy, even in hard seasons.

Daily Affirmation

I give myself grace for the days that feel heavy.

What's On My Heart Today?

Daily Affirmation

I am not alone in this journey—support surrounds me.

What's On My Heart Today?

Daily Affirmation

I trust myself to make the best decisions with what I know today.

What's On My Heart Today?

Daily Affirmation

Even in service to others, I am allowed to protect my peace.

What's On My Heart Today?

Daily Affirmation

I can pause. I can breathe. I can begin again.

What's On My Heart Today?

Daily Affirmation

My caregiving does not have to come at the cost of myself.

What's On My Heart Today?

Daily Affirmation

I honor the sacred work I do, even when no one sees it.

What's On My Heart Today?

Daily Affirmation

It's okay to ask for more support—
I don't have to do it all.

What's On My Heart Today?

Daily Affirmation

My worth is not defined by how much I produce or fix.

What's On My Heart Today?

Daily Affirmation

I give myself permission to feel everything—without judgment.

What's On My Heart Today?

Daily Affirmation

Today, I choose compassion—for them and for myself.

What's On My Heart Today?

Daily Affirmation

 My needs matter, even when others are depending on me.

What's On My Heart Today?

Daily Affirmation

 I am doing the best I can—and that is enough.

What's On My Heart Today?

Daily Affirmation

It is safe for me to slow down and be still.

What's On My Heart Today?

Daily Affirmation

I honor the version of me that is tired and still trying.

What's On My Heart Today?

Daily Affirmation

Joy is still possible in the middle of this.

What's On My Heart Today?

Daily Affirmation

Every part of me deserves gentleness—including the weary parts.

What's On My Heart Today?

Daily Affirmation

I can carry love and still need space.

What's On My Heart Today?

Daily Affirmation

Today, I will breathe before I break.

What's On My Heart Today?

Daily Affirmation

Even when I feel unseen, I am still whole.

What's On My Heart Today?

Daily Affirmation

My presence is enough. I am enough.

What's On My Heart Today?

Daily Affirmation

I give myself permission to rest without guilt.

What's On My Heart Today?

Daily Affirmation

Peace begins with one breath.

What's On My Heart Today?

Daily Affirmation

I deserve the same compassion I offer others.

What's On My Heart Today?

Daily Affirmation

It's okay to feel joy, even on the hard days.

What's On My Heart Today?

Daily Affirmation

My love is enough, even when I feel like I'm not.

What's On My Heart Today?

Daily Affirmation

Slowing down is a sacred act of self-preservation.

What's On My Heart Today?

Daily Affirmation

I am not required to be everything to everyone.

What's On My Heart Today?

Daily Affirmation

Grief and gratitude can coexist in my heart.

What's On My Heart Today?

Daily Affirmation

My story is still being written, and I am the author.

What's On My Heart Today?

Daily Affirmation

I welcome healing in my own time and way.

What's On My Heart Today?

Daily Affirmation

I am worthy of being cared for too.

What's On My Heart Today?

Daily Affirmation

I choose grace over perfection today.

What's On My Heart Today?

Daily Affirmation

Even small acts of self-care are sacred.

What's On My Heart Today?

Daily Affirmation

My needs are not a burden—they are valid.

What's On My Heart Today?

Daily Affirmation

I release what I cannot control.

What's On My Heart Today?

Daily Affirmation

There is power in my pause.

What's On My Heart Today?

Daily Affirmation

I am learning to let joy back in.

What's On My Heart Today?

Daily Affirmation

I can care deeply for others without abandoning myself.

What's On My Heart Today?

Daily Affirmation

I honor the quiet strength within me.

What's On My Heart Today?

Daily Affirmation

Today, I will move at the pace of grace.

What's On My Heart Today?

Daily Affirmation

I choose to be kind to myself today.

What's On My Heart Today?

Daily Affirmation

My rest is just as sacred as my service.

What's On My Heart Today?

Daily Affirmation

I welcome softness in the middle of this hard.

What's On My Heart Today?

Daily Affirmation

Even on the hardest days, I am still enough.

What's On My Heart Today?

Daily Affirmation

It's okay to need help and still be strong.

What's On My Heart Today?

Daily Affirmation

I give myself permission to be human.

What's On My Heart Today?

Daily Affirmation

My story is sacred, even when it's messy.

What's On My Heart Today?

Daily Affirmation

I am not alone in this journey.

What's On My Heart Today?

Daily Affirmation

○ I am growing even when it feels like surviving.

What's On My Heart Today?

Daily Affirmation

○ Today, I honor how far I've come.

What's On My Heart Today?

Daily Affirmation

Today, I will move at the pace of grace.

What's On My Heart Today?

Daily Affirmation

I am no longer abandoning myself to hold others together.

What's On My Heart Today?

Daily Affirmation

My needs are not a burden—they are sacred.

What's On My Heart Today?

Daily Affirmation

I am learning to receive the same love I so freely give.

What's On My Heart Today?

Daily Affirmation

Every gentle choice I make for myself is an act of healing.

What's On My Heart Today?

Daily Affirmation

I release the weight of guilt and invite in grace.

What's On My Heart Today?

Daily Affirmation

My body, my spirit, and my story deserve tenderness.

What's On My Heart Today?

Daily Affirmation

I am slowly becoming someone I trust.

What's On My Heart Today?

Daily Affirmation

Peace is not a place I go to—it's what I create within.

What's On My Heart Today?

Daily Affirmation

I am reclaiming my joy without apology.

What's On My Heart Today?

Daily Affirmation

Today, I will move at the pace of grace.

What's On My Heart Today?

Daily Affirmation

I am no longer abandoning myself to hold others together.

What's On My Heart Today?

Daily Affirmation

My needs are not a burden—they are sacred.

What's On My Heart Today?

Daily Affirmation

I am learning to receive the same love I so freely give.

What's On My Heart Today?

Daily Affirmation

Every gentle choice I make for myself is an act of healing.

What's On My Heart Today?

Daily Affirmation

I release the weight of guilt and invite in grace.

What's On My Heart Today?

Daily Affirmation

My body, my spirit, and my story deserve tenderness.

What's On My Heart Today?

Daily Affirmation

I am slowly becoming someone I trust.

What's On My Heart Today?

Daily Affirmation

Peace is not a place I go to—it's what I create within.

What's On My Heart Today?

Daily Affirmation

I am reclaiming my joy without apology.

What's On My Heart Today?

Daily Affirmation

I give myself permission to heal at my own pace.

What's On My Heart Today?

Daily Affirmation

My presence is a gift, even when I am silent.

What's On My Heart Today?

Daily Affirmation

I deserve gentleness from myself and others.

What's On My Heart Today?

Daily Affirmation

It is okay to rest. I am still enough when I pause.

What's On My Heart Today?

Daily Affirmation

Each breath I take is a new beginning.

What's On My Heart Today?

Daily Affirmation

I can love fully without losing myself.

What's On My Heart Today?

Daily Affirmation

I honor the woman I was and the one I'm becoming.

What's On My Heart Today?

Daily Affirmation

My boundaries are sacred, and they protect my peace.

What's On My Heart Today?

Daily Affirmation

Joy still lives inside me—I choose to notice it today.

What's On My Heart Today?

Daily Affirmation

I can ask for help and still be strong.

What's On My Heart Today?

Daily Affirmation

My healing matters, even if no one else sees it.

What's On My Heart Today?

Daily Affirmation

Today, I choose grace over pressure.

What's On My Heart Today?

Daily Affirmation

I am not alone—my strength walks beside me.

What's On My Heart Today?

Daily Affirmation

It's okay to not have all the answers.

What's On My Heart Today?

Daily Affirmation

My peace is a priority, not an afterthought.

What's On My Heart Today?

Daily Affirmation

Each day I care, I grow deeper in compassion—for others and myself.

What's On My Heart Today?

Daily Affirmation

There is no shame in needing support.

What's On My Heart Today?

Daily Affirmation

My story is worthy of being told.

What's On My Heart Today?

Daily Affirmation

Healing doesn't mean forgetting—it means remembering with peace.

What's On My Heart Today?

Daily Affirmation

I offer myself the same patience I give others.

What's On My Heart Today?

Daily Affirmation

○ It's brave to feel deeply and still keep going.

What's On My Heart Today?

Daily Affirmation

○ I am rediscovering the beauty of my own presence.

What's On My Heart Today?

Daily Affirmation

Today, I honor how far I've come.

What's On My Heart Today?

Daily Affirmation

My boundaries teach others how to love me better.

What's On My Heart Today?

Daily Affirmation

I give myself room to cry, to breathe, and to rise.

What's On My Heart Today?

Daily Affirmation

My softness is not weakness—it is wisdom.

What's On My Heart Today?

Daily Affirmation

Peace begins with a single exhale.

What's On My Heart Today?

Daily Affirmation

I deserve to be poured into, not just poured from.

What's On My Heart Today?

Daily Affirmation

Even in silence, I am worthy of love and care.

What's On My Heart Today?

Daily Affirmation

Each step I take toward healing is a sacred act of courage.

What's On My Heart Today?

Open Space To Share Your Thoughts

www.ingramcontent.com/pod-product-compliance
Lightning Source LLC
LaVergne TN
LVHW061531070526
838199LV00010B/454